dreams & dissent

dreams & dissent

NEW POEMS, 1961-1970

by george abbe

NOONE HOUSE, PETERBOROUGH, NEW HAMPSHIRE

WILLIAM L. BAUHAN, PUBLISHER

contents

part

From the Fields Below

I cannot say what robin answered me, but there was one
last-twilight, dark-descending one
that spoke across the hawthorns' fading flowers,
the dying white of shadblow dusky-falling.

I heard that murmur of the robin's talk,
last words that spoke, past hawthorn white,
beyond the shrubby dogwood's lingering brightness —
brief words out of swelling fragrant pause
before the day became the utter night.

I cannot say which bird, but I am sure
he sought to reach me with language more than birds' —
for he had seen me pass and knew my speech
was such as love addresses to mate and child;
and so, recalling, he spoke a fragment to me —

love's half-unconscious hope and desperate denial
of that recurring inconceivable death of day.

The Lamb

I stabbed
a lamb. The knife made
a straight brightness downward, in one slow
blow; it went through fat that seemed
deep, unendingly deep. In fainting horror
I saw that no blood came.

The body gave to the impact;
the lamb regarded me
evenly, composedly — curious, as though expecting
an accusation. I waited for blood
to come. There was none.

The lamb moved slowly; it went down in a courteous
unburdening of life; it settled
in gentleness,
correctly, its gaze unmoving.
I knew only that there was no blood
through all the fat.

Kingbirds Topple
Backward in Mid-Air

Going along the blown brown tips of grasses,
I was walking the flimmer foam the flemling suds of brown;
I heard an aching fiddle-flur, a rip of fleecy voices,
a vagrant and belleneal blue of moving love.

It was the kingbird dappering on a tip of pear tree,
cleeping and peri-totting to his young
all bundled in a nest of twig and twine and sun.

Then he climbed suddenly
far up and fell backward,
O almost motionless on his back — toppled and lay,
then hugged himself up close and tumbled forward again,
nickling and boddling in ecstatic wonder,
float-drummling down to the pear-tree tip again,

hung there, wings a-jimmer, talked to wife,
who up-weaving and bloony, hundled and tripled in a web of wind.

And this, all this because the young were fed
and living, and fed and fat,
within the green-shuttered boughs, so close below;

and blouncy day cried water and shade and strum
of creatures breathing and wallacking over wingle of earth,
the froth of love.

And I, sliding on grass-tips, the kingbirds tipping the noon-tree,
all tindering and sprawning high,
became a brother-tug, a deathless play and affection.

Young Marriage
and the Ski-Run

Have you seen that year return
whose lean fox heart beat
clean the frozen vein of loss?

Toss of the snow hills out of the fist of sun.
I shot down slopes more sheer than thought.
At bottom, chaos fell.
Too full with white, the valley, bending,
rent downward into void;
the reeling ski snapped up, the heel
of knowledge breaking hard.

Over the gulf I spun,
undone from human means and motive;
lonely the farmland buildings small below;
and folded in monstrous speed,
weaned from the nipple of all past,
I tasted succulent milk of lust,
the gusty passion of all outer space.

Till, tumbling face down, stretching
flesh, essaying to touch the rocks recalled,
                    dim rivers,
tips of firs like dazzled motes
in flowing light of distance and cold, I felt
the lonely helplessness of stars, of God, until
the frail brown of a dot, a dwelling

like seed-shell broke; from mortal windows woke
a flake of vision, white; your raised
face as remembered grew,
drawing me back to tangency and place,
blest sorrow of time,
the winding torrents of doubt, the flesh
blind as the glancing speed
of skis, all bound in fury and fear
of early loving.

I fell, and saw the violent and crude
news of the earth rush up
to fire my tongue, to canonize
my mind.

The Spoon

Taste bud
and thought divine
flower as well in silver or blood,
whirl on the vein or in metallic shine
that lives as rich as man, as ripe with good
and just as prone to hope, as able
to sing by giving, to touch,
respond, make table
or mouth thrive.

Below
table and floor
soil burns, fires flow
out of which my image is born;
and now I long to stretch the hand
of memory, retake and know
what passion I let go, or
failed to understand
in that deep
land.

Yet
at times,
caught by the sound
of woman singing at work,
my roots break, joy stirs and climbs
out of my subtle dark,
my exile wound:
Her passion
is mine.

October's End:
A Roman in the Oak

Below me on the heath-wild slopes
a huge oak drunk with final pride
watches the great hills' paling glow
and fiercer burns, more furious cries.

O blackened wind of living hues
that blew into this single oak,
you were a Roman, dead at a blow,
who bled in dark, and then awoke;

You were the courtly strong who stepped
up stairs of stone in the ringing years.
In Hippodromes deep under death
you drove the black horses of the stars.

O long-sustained, unyielding tree,
your glory is that stoic man
who teaches that as we shall die
so also shall we be again.

The Age of Snow

The tunnel of snow went down. We carried guns.
Sun half came through.
The blue of light sang at our flattened skin
like the crooning of whips. The raw pale
white opened to tearing hands.

I called; I called in the searing air:
"Paula! . . . Paula . . . !" The turns
curved hard and deep
like sleeping veins of moons
in worlds of ether
dreamed before our coming.

"Paula! . . . Paula!" The ice
showed blood from our feet now bare.

Abruptly, trunk of a tree
sank roots across our way,
flaring and rank with earth
long buried, nearly forgotten, under
thunderous ages of snow.

I stood back to fire,
to tear the wood asunder
with gun.

But there, at the base —
a dead squirrel, frail and staring, the fur
sparkled with rime,

creature from wilds before the Age of White,
who had endured a while at the wood's core.

And up the trunk we stared; and past the snow,
through cave-ins opening high, the living blue
of time, and air, above the continental cold.
Then only did our mortal passion,
memory of hoping, die in our flesh.
"Paula!" I breathed again; but knew
that if the feminine and lovable,
last symbol to give strength
had gone this way,
then like the animal
she must have perished too.

The Natural Man
and the Instrument Panel

He walked from the next town
because he liked the air:
the trees were easy friends,
the true rock was there.
He scorned men in machines
as escaping self through speed.

Yet hour by hour the sky
from straight ahead closed down
like a plane cockpit panel
flashing unbearable sun;

dials whirled in polished fire,
the meter pointers screamed;
key slits were crooked traps
in which the hills were maimed.

The mathematic drone
quivered the gauges' glass;
from scientific arch
peered numbers without rust.

To south and west the same —
the air was gone, the air!
He held the cockpit now:
the instruments shone clear,
sharp ready to his hand,
and speed, and speed was his,
if he would pause and note,
if he would yield and seize.

Yet all, all the long slopes,
where he had walked, had waned —
he, the glad walker, the lover
of bark, and the harsh ground!

Maddened, spinning about,
he struck the panel glass,
and knew, as his bones broke,
that he struck his own blind flesh.

His leisure, others' haste
met at cross-hairs of the crash.

Summer Decision

I would prefer
to word my final phrase
in the blaze of swallow blue, the crying
brightness of bugloss fields' dark-towering, burning blue.

I would choose
to do the final deed
of bleeding, or heroic madness,
or sacrifice, in the sheen of hawkweed gold.

For without them
I am negated. Coiled
in the roiling, gentle, sudden, drifting
vividness of their contentment I survive.

Their spontaneous thought,
the somberness which veins
their prayer for darkness or rain,
are mine for personal rendering of our singleness,
our mutual immortality.

What Keeps the Lovers
in the Trees Below?

Pure day that lately brought me tides of boughs
and blossoms all too dark with the rain's sleep,
what keeps the lovers in the trees below,
what scent of warmth is far too false and deep?

The birds that weave the metal mesh of flight
bring down that gleaming snare upon what head?
And though the lovers, hidden, fumble and cry,
can there be flesh that learns, or thirsting, bends?

Come up, come up that hill of crumbled stone
where the thorn races red upon the sun's sea;
the blossomed bush dies before seed is born,
the smoke from chimneys shrouds the gravestone's eye.

What could they find even if they tore
the arm, the breast from brambles below day,
and out of shadow sprang, and upward bore
the templed throat, the brow of certainty? —

Only this hill, with blossoms choking in sun;
only this steeple, empty of all save past,
the equal grave, the harbor of locust thorn,
and air too hot with death for lovers' thirst.

The Examination

A drab,
unhappy, piteous
little bird rose stiff
and still out of a ball of snow.
Below the visible white roundness, his legs

descended
invisibly to somewhere.
And then he struggled. The snow
broke open; I saw an owl gripping
the thin, thread-like lines of his legs, holding him

implacably
in the trap of his claws.
Some law, I realized, said
he could never escape. Then I grew aware
I was there to take an examination. I stood

bloodless and weak, and stared at what
I must be questioned about, and knew
the law would elude me forever,
as inexorably as the owl
would hold the frozen,
thin, black threads
of the bird's legs.

The Ferns Beneath

Where gnomes beneath the earth converse with darkness
and touch the living sounds of winds long gone,
the living ferns of hope burn with a sun
fierce and immortal, taller than all man's madness
and stronger than all the history that is done.
Break upward, dwarfs of dark that weave our future
out of the ore of gods locked in our past;
strike the green ferns of angriest redemption
taller than city, taller than last bomb blast.
For everything satanic and profane
that man abandoned in deeper, innocent soil,
that cried that love sweet and irrational,
shall burst to greenness richer than all that fails,
shall curve the temple of faith of nobler men
across that sky where birds outspeed our lust,
and the rain falls, simple and innocent,
and love, like the ferns, towers beyond our dust,
as wild as the ferment of the stars, and never spent.

The Caterpillar

I lay upon the soft of day,
the green of bounty shyly known.
The light came through my windows free,
the branches of my trust were plain,
fretting a bronzed and cordial sky.

All, all about me, people went
at duties that would make me safe;
their strength was my astonishment;
and, godly, they knew no mistake.

But all at once, the couch, the room
broke outward to the sweltering lawn;
the floors for treasured footsteps waned,
the walls whose bright designs were drawn
by innocence, sank without sound.

I placed my hand on the lush grass:
under it, suffocating calm
beat like the shadow of a wound;
the heat, upwavering to my bone,
fused me to coil of ugliness.

And there, in a fold of the lawn's flesh,
scar from a careless human heel,
a caterpillar, hued intense,
unwound from earth, uprose immense,
loomed over me and numbed my gaze,
its glistening rank with pleasuring.

And now, the sun dimmed; high and thick
from hill to hill, from house to house,
a bagworm tent strung huge and course;
within its gray the worms writhed black;
flickered its surface with coiling young;
heavy as breast it strove to break;
the air grew vile; the sun was gone.

And I must lift into that nest,
to safety inviolate and warm,
companioned dense to smother pain,
this caterpillar sly with charm.

I must persuade where he could loll,
and I protect that rapture faint
with softness like the rooms within
the very house where I had lain.

Your Profile
in This Desperate Hour

Your profile against this grieving light,
lifted and elegant and flowing,
is like that oriole whose cries
honeyed my shadowy schoolboy days
with ardor rounded as love's undoing.

The lawn up-tilted to maples' domain
a flying carpet flung to take
that gentle prince of journeying sound,
breath of the sun and the sorrowing wind.
So now, half shadowed, half in pain,
your profile speaks the spaceless mind.

Over and over like child in hay,
rolling in saffron and dusky blue,
that impulse velvet with gaiety.
And from hair to forehead to quick eyes now
tumbles in outline that beautiful news
that a full love utters in hidden boughs.

To an Ancient Lady I Loved

Down air of listening, lake under mountain,
late fell that loon call, hung
wondrous above your home.

I saw the fir tips, boat above image,
mist of the evening, and you, lady,
aged, and I the child.

You walked the shore needles, frail and bright,
kindness you slipped like rope rings outward;
doubt-free I moved, I rowed.

All that my young heart treasured, perceived,
was bleeding of night from wing of the evening,
lean tremor and hunger of loon.

All that I knew was your carved smile
riding from sources different from storm of breast.
I fed at your lips, braver.

Wisdom and wryness, the pale humor poised,
knowing no offspring, husband, ready
for dying, the last humble grief.

To reach my hand — if I could have touched;
but such was the boat, the mist-long shadow,
the sad, ineffable loon,

I drew at oars only, and saw
hewn at the neck by mist, your face,
gracious and terrible, smiling;

and light, upward light, yet weighted as death
to loon voice shudder, the mountain rising
merely to die, to fail. . . .

But haste of my oars, my muscles' drive!
Living! to live! I took from you courage,
words unspoken for speed,

while you
must dim to the speechless,
must lean backward out of the boat
to float downward with mountain and loon.

The Lark and the Aster

To drift, demented, in white fields of asters!
Look up, look up! Sky's indigo
and sun are spinning like a copper pail
of water whirled centrifugal.
White asters — gnarled and knotted snow —
catch at my knees and tear me wild.

And there's the prairie lark! From winter drifts
I saved it when its wing hung torn,
and housed it. Through the zero winds
her mate rose up and belled his cry
winter-long.
                    In spring, I let her go.
In ledge-shale nest, four larks were born.
Open to hawks. I guarded them close.

This zest, this sensing, this stone-sharp joy
in what I've given and pluck from flight
of days — this flings me arrowed away
to a house I came upon when skiing
in a harsh, storm-coming gloom of light
on woods downy with owl's plaint,
and the fox gone, and the pheasant afraid.

It was a summer house. The screens
of porch and window hummed with wind.
First flicks of snow sifted within.
Chairs toppling; yellow fireplace wood
hunched in a dubious reverie;

the dirt beneath the porch asleep
with toy and shovel and burnt match, gray
with glimmer of tin-foil, scraps of bread.

And they were vanished — whatever had moved
at center, whatever touched and fed.
The stairway was pinched like a lover that's starved;
blown snow against panes spoke caresses dead.

Now here, here in autumn, in asters crazed
with that crooked and terrible vigor of rapture,
and light on the larks that are gods to my need,
I know that something stands empty and stunned,
the wood still unburned, and the stairs of my blood
stricken; these moments, like scattered bread
under the porch facing beauty's sun.

The screening whines with the first fierce brood
of cold that was warmth and of pity made pain;
the savior I was and the saved that I loved
housed in waiting, in absence, the fire and the flown.

part 2

My Father's Death

The rain was relentless and whole.
The cold-sodden streets were strung
like shiny gut between sinews
of trees. Like a skid-row
the bars and tenements tilted
over crowds of men
hunched, waiting, in rain.

Waiting? How long? And why?
Why was my father there?
Severe, respectable,
full of patient sorrow
all his life — why now
in this crowd of panhandlers, did he stand
gaunt, lofty, and silent?

And then I saw he wore rubber
the others lacked: thick coat,
slick, warm boots, black hat
jutting past tragic brow.

A slow, wistful look of pleasure;
an expectancy half-plaintive;
so long remorseful, so long half-trusting.
Fleshed now in rubber, secure.
Never before as safe.
Through rain he confidently moved.
My love tore like a shock.
I saw he carried a brief-case

cold flaming wet, of black
thick rubber — containing a dry
shyness of years, a message
groping and frail,
remembered only
by himself.

"How difficult is faith when Christ died
so long ago, and never has returned,"
remarked my friend. "It may be," I replied,
"and yet he does come back, I have just learned.

In that intense cold of the coldest day,
between sunset and dark when the west is a rose shade
and quiet lies on the palm of the air,
the infinite rounded hills swing out, yet near,
I climbed toward home, fighting snow to my knees,
with each step praising God, with each step praying
for the hunted creatures in their tunnelled dark.
I sang, jubilant because no dog
had left a trace of killing where I'd walked.

And blessing God for each lungful of hard
terrible cold because it made life alert,
I struggled toward my ridge and homecoming warmth,
yet eager to stay on the piercing meadows of search.

And suddenly, heavy and tragic, yet burdenless
as love's pain, a bird winged slowly over my path —
an owl, whose thoughtful flight contains the grace
we cannot reach perhaps, yet strive to, with faith
too cumbersome, too bound by evil's flesh.

He flew ahead. I yearned to see his face.
How easily yet remorseful against
that burning pang of twilight blue he leaned —
level and bowed, as though his thoughts were blessed
by knowledge I could never truly reach.

And over, directly over my lonely house
he sailed, and settled on the single pole
that holds our wires for lights and telephone;
and there, in deepening night, over naked fields
where the mice burrow that I love and long to shield
from hawk and dog, he perched, utterly lone,
utterly still. I watched to catch some thrill
of wakened movement, some serene lift
of head. Nothing. The dark shape cold
and muffled, like the pole's top, hooded and stiff,
clung against western glow; darkened, blurred
into the dimming, ethereal blue of icy night,
till my straining eyes confused pole and bird.
He seemed to move a little only because my sight
wavered from fixedness. No sound. No turn
of head. No plunge to snatch pipit or mouse.

With shock, I knew Christ was that bird,
visiting me in the warm and hooded head
to watch over my dwelling while I slept
under the flame-cold blue arcing the world's prayer.
He broods perceptive, forming me later words;
he thinks the acts that out of sleep I'll dare;
his patience to conclude will break my fear,
teach me when to be still, and when to curve
down from dark height in necessity's calm rush,
with gentle softness as downy as God's wish.

I lay
in a strange house,
in a downy, deep, monstrous bed. The walls
fell outward; the ceiling withdrew
like a wounded beast. Everything
was big around me. I lay small.

                          Then a sound
was aroused like a canyon's dead
echo — a footstep,
measured, foreboding. A robber,
undoubtedly. Paralyzed, I stretched
under the heavy, silken quilt. The steps came
straight, unerring toward the bed.

Then the round beam of a flashlight fluttered and fell
like a gentle, calm, wide snowflake —
and remained fixed — in the exact center
of my chest — precisely where the dull,
pulling pains of indigestion always recurred.

Deep-buried, cold, unmoving, the room ceased
breathing in the outward-collapsing dark. And I lay
waiting for that leap.
                    But only
that glow, soft and light, seemed to bless
my chest in the exact center.

The Mortal Traveller

A man swung eastward
through poplars' gold;
dust on the leaf-tips;
crickets called.

Kingfisher's shadow;
stream below sand;
crows over meadows;
taut hills beyond.

Long fell the noon-light,
late lay the chill
between sunset and night,
past footfall and shoal.

But straight along roadway,
parting the air,
a man moved with heartbeat,
his muscles sure.

An owl drifted slowly;
the doors of the wind
swung wide to admit
that visioning mind

like a finger stretched
from thought to form,
to house past hill-curve,
the unseen made home.

Not people, not the dying
frightened milling of human cities
flicks the dial of my heart to prayer.

I pray no more for man.
Blasted by his own science, the evil
steaming in the geysers of precise loveless

study and competence,
he bends and fails, he suffocates
in the gray bubbling of his degeneracy.

Instead,
I press the broken twig
to wish it healing in a further
world; I touch the bud to urge its noblest

growing; the mosses brown
with drought I spread my palm upon
that rain may sooner sting their tips with green

once more. I stand at night
beside a sapling rooted in stark
rock, holding it gently firm, to warm

it toward its future; its pulse
runs into mine. "Strong, living friend,
bend the great sky to your joy," I say.

And glad I cry: "Praise Christ!
For why deplore what man has wanted,
sought with all his blue prints, cleverness, machines,

his resource, comfort, ideals
beaten into the image of dollar
and rockets bearing the same dead power to moons?

Why sorrow for his death
set in that changeless arrogance?
Rather, turn to the simple, innocent, and good,

and pray for that. Unite
the fighting uniqueness of your heart,
the sparkling intuitive mind with vital nature.

Pray for it, its wise,
fine, incorruptible vigor,
the lift and throb of its God. Pray, pray."

I focus pitying thought
on moth, ant, cricket, fledgling, fern;
I yearn God's beam of blessing down on hawk and worm.

The poplar sapling crushed
by truck, the eager shagbark shoot
the boot of man has snapped, I set erect

and bind, and wish the sap
back through its stoic, reverent
flesh. I cup the window-glass-stunned bird

and warm it back to flight;
the just-alighted fly, buzzing in gluey
doom, I pinch to snuff his torment out.

I radiate to rocks
my longing for their deep fruition.
Swift grace of cloud or swallow I draw

an aura of prayer around;
the sounding friendship of rivers I reach
with leaping hope for God's down-streaming care.

And thus, while desolation
ranges man's world, foretelling extinction,
quickening the bloated madness that will burst,

I break through time to spur
the miracle of natural fortune and growth,
the closing of distance between all innocent things

and their targets set by God,
the strong fulfillments prayer can speed,
speech that here began as elusive communion,

sound-symbol, psychic flash,
but at last, out there, as communication
blazing-clear, will shape inconceivable structures of color,

cathedrals of harmonic power,
the towering praises our prayers of earth
gave birth to, girded, prepared by touch, inarticulate love,

the trusting word,
the lone, inadequate thrust of hope
toward the incorruptible.

The Ski Jumper
Who Died Before Me

I heard last night the voice of one
long gone before me into air,
whose ample heart rolled with the sun,
whose wrist beat with the comet's cheer;
and on his brow the youthful snows
whose strength he'd matched with straining limb
whirled in amazed arpeggios;
his shoulders arched a furious hymn
from cloudy moon to asteroid.
For ski poles he had gripped askew
great shafts of light through sundered void.

Down slopes too terrible to know
he schussed, and outward sprang, and poised
before my shocked and upward gaze.
"What are you now?" I heard my voice.
"There in mid-leap your sinews freeze;
your eyes are cindered blind with haste
unfinished and immeasurable."

"And did you," came that tone from space,
"believe that I control my fall
because I live past mortal time
and wear some strange, heroic law?
My virtue pauses at your shame,
my beauty hesitates with yours;
my feet will find the landing slope,
that crystal, sensate glide of power,

when you bring down your Titan hope
from wish to wide creation *there* —

arched purpose that your conscience woke
flashing to levels tall ablaze
with roofs more cleansed than Holy Grail
and brothers thronging shouts of praise."

Messiah

Today, on the city's skyline,
I welcomed the hero of peoples,
his heart the flung arc of the rivet
beating white behind ribs of girders;
his eye the airplane's needle
of light over smoke-cliff and harbor.

He strode, and his stride was the echoed
wonder of trucks in chasms;
his knee was the piston of taxis,
his belt the jeweler's prism;
his hands swung supple as trees
in the parkways thickened by summer;
he reached with the fingers of buses;
he preached with the subway's thunder.

Buildings broke open like pumpkins;
the seeds of voices slid golden.
I smelled the split soul of man's growing;
I walked in the pulp of the moment.

And huge though this Master moved,
and valiant in all his fibre,
more valiant I found my blood,
more herculean my labor;
for all my pleasures were his,
and I was redeemed by being
entire in the thrust of his lung,
complete in the core of his seeing.

For I am the child of my city,
yet father of all it gives;
its breath is my martyred hoping;
its pride is my body that loves;
and all of its lust and boasting
is that godly, articulate joy
shaping the deathless for doubters,
immense eschatology
before which our guilt is broken,
upon which we ceaselessly pour
prayer for the act of excitement,
praise for the fact we endure.

The Meat

Each day I see in my meat the beast that died
that I may stand and pump my blood.
Each bud of sweetness is his branch of pain;
my praise of taste and life
the singing blossoms strung
along his strength which went down under the club,
wondering, struck, which hung astonished, lashed
with anguish, conscious, chained, head down.

Each hour I walk, I think of flesh in mine
like wine bursting a grape-skin, poured into me
by bleeding which was innocence, by terror amazed,
by crazed awareness that the ones
most trusted were betraying, the feeders opening
the throat they'd fed.

Remembering this, my morning joy turns cold.
That crowd of deep, warm, singing corpuscles I feel
once healed and gladdened and made calm the beast.
He yielded them to me.
Now they accuse and question all my good.

Frail Is That Road

Frail is that road
like lint upon the sun
that in the noon will burn,
will crisp and curl
and infinitely turn
into itself.

Frail is the creature
breathing on its white,
the speck of man
who faster runs
and wonders what
that spasm is that pulls
the road beyond his hand.

The Unfailing

I am not fast enough in closing
        the screen door behind me: a moth flutters in,
climbs to the ceiling, blunders
           down inside the lamp-shade. When I
                  try to catch it,
it eludes me, flies under the couch. I give up.

The next morning, I see it on
        the tile wall of the bathroom.
           Again I pursue. It would be easy
to crush it, but I have an intuitive
        belief all things are equally important;
their basic functions — eating, sleeping, playing,
protecting their young, contemplating —
           are the same; and I recall Blake's words:

    "Kill not the moth or butterfly;
    For the Last Judgement draweth nigh."

So I persist. I place my handkerchief
        swiftly and gently over the moth;
but when I
      try to pick it up, carefully, considerately,
           it slips away; when I
                finally
get it into the living-room and out the door, I
           find it does
             not emerge
from my handkerchief when I open
        it. Going back, I
           find it on the floor, still
             uninjured.

This time, my tender enclosing and lifting

                    trap it securely. On the front steps,

opening my handkerchief again,

          I see the brown, gold-barred insect zoom away.

In another

    country, many lives distant from

              this one, I am climbing a vast

                    lonely slanting shelf of land

like a raised beach

    from which the surf of a million years

              has receded.

              I see

the bones of colossal dead fish, the skeletons of animals like dino-

  saurs, the wreckage of ships. Over everything

            rests

          a gentle, ominous stillness.

I am desperately tired, and I am seeking

          to reach a truth beyond the cliff

                that lifts at

the horizon's edge. In this region, it is not food or shelter one

                  attains, not

a conquest of safety or power, but fresh

          perception — revelation like sudden

star-splinters, a white maelstrom sprung

          abruptly against the terrace windows

                of the mind.

I feel that I shall glimpse a verity beyond the beach,
                              the searing hot
                              rim of rock
                                    that shocks into blue
distance and falling
                bodies of gulls that come over,
                              come over endlessly,
                                    pleading for life again,
for food no longer present on dark, frothing waves, for this conti-
nent has gone dry.

I struggle
      upward along the blistering sand; the sun
                              blunts its searing edge
on my shoulder. I feel strength going;
                        the flow of sweat
                        gives me the sensation
of being sucked into a water-shaft of death.
                              And then, abruptly, the shelf
of beach begins
      to give way, to crumble. I slip downward into a gaping crevasse;
fear erupts like a volcano flame and lava against the dome of my
      mind. I cry out
and grope at the sandy margins of the fissure.
                        But I slide deeper.

Then, over me glides the brown, gold-barred moth I had spared
      and taken to the outdoor light. It dips
                        and tilts as though examining me. I hear
its voice, piping and thin; and the words, strangely, are instantly
                                          intelligible.
I realize that in my earlier life they had been
                        too high-pitched for me to catch.
Now, he is telling me to let go, to trust.

I recognize him as the moth
                    of that earthly time, and I obey. At first,
the loosening of my grip plummets me into smothering blackness;
                                                but then
                                                        I sense
the moth's wings curved against my side,
                                    light and electric with power.
I feel them tighten, subtly, and then lift.

I am carried to the light, the beach again;
                        I am borne up
                                over the skeletons
and the flotsam toward the cliff's
                        rim. And there,
                                looking over and down
and far out, I perceive
            the new meaning.

Jesus Changing and Returning

Jesus crossed the square;
he walked the vast debris,
the tangled wreckage poured
like rubbish from the sky.

And what I noticed first —
he did not seem to be
like stories I had heard
nor pictures I had seen.

Energy lashed his brow
and whipped the willing mouth;
impatience gripped his eye
like eagle's glinting claw;

He leaned a trifle out
toward action and the need
like boulders poised to drop
toward valleys dimly deep;

and quick on muscled neck
the head turned, scenting the scene
like big guns probing the thick
cold rain of flailing shot.

No meekness in that cheek,
but hard and rugged chance;
the rebel slash of thought
toward man's deliverance
from ages sold and bought
to keep the humble weak.

I looked to see the scars
flame in the prisoned palms;
but they were opened clear,
calloused and unashamed,
from tool and bruising shock.
The only wounds they bore
were revolution's name.

The square was mordant-still;
poisonous dust-fumes hung
like smoke from a rock-drill
rising on lifeless wing
over a monstrous hill.

Breathing with even zest,
he came and faced me full,
the tendons of his neck
strung like a muted blast
of music in heaven's hall,
and stretching his hand, exclaimed:
"What darkness struck your earth?"

His touch was harshly grave,
a fierce and warming urge,
allegiance firmly serene.

I felt a rush of the brave.

"Broken," I said, "and riven
by the bolted lust of the mind
shaped to the missile driven
out of the rotting wind
that rises from human pride."

He nodded; his eye drove clean
into my bone and brain.
"We are brothers," he said.
"You know the cruel must be done;
that only hurt can change,
can twist the foul to the good."

"We need a different Jesus,"
I replied. "You have been nailed
on walls and bled to wine,
shaped to the withered and frail."
I waved my hand at the square,
the subway trains thrust forth
mangled and shattered, half hurled
out of their tunnelled earth
and crumbled in rubble of towers.

"There," I said, "is the deed
of those who depicted you pale,
crucified, writhing, sad,
who built our churches' power,
preached the good and the bad,
cowed us with sacred fears."

"Yes, there," he said, "is the act
of those who made me a shrine,
ritual rather than fact
that glows and beats in the mind,
different for every man."

My heart leaped. "Glorious one,
I sensed you under the gloom
of conformity weighting the bone,
machinery racking the blood,
but never believed you would come
into the open hour,
the blazing world of the flesh
where our senses teach us the pure
and the only vision is wish.
And yet . . ." My heart surged hot
and a drumbeat unleashed my lips.
". . . you are here. Will you die? Will you fight
for what you abandoned before? —
a strength in the fibre of Now,
a masculine, generous Here?"

He smiled, and breathed the air
of that dead city; it shone
like a gray corpse suddenly washed.

"I was not piteous and queer;
I fought. Yes, I was alone.
My disciples tried, and were crushed.
I remained bold, and I bled.
I ripped the pretense from wrong,
I broke the conventional good;
my energy rampaged and sang;
my love was assertion's rush
flooding the daily forlorn,
the common, the simpler thing.

I hated the rich and the lush,
I raged at the righteously strong.
And when they nailed me up,
I stretched, and I defied;
I declared God's deathless cheer
till my pulse broke, and I died."

"Did they gamble for your robe?"

"I had none."
             "Did they take
your body to a friend's tomb?"

"They may have. I do not know.
But it's sure they did not come
to pluck me from my fate.
They were too busy being
like the institutions that cut
the euphoria out of my heart,
like organized man that wrung
the ebullience out of my veins,
like the customary-secure
that equate evil with pain
and maunder of sin to prevent
the revelation of change."

The Influence

Flashing
dots and dashes from former lives, from every earlier
person who influenced me, I walk,
talk, do, in this new
existence; I am the telegraphic
impact and language
of all words, ideas, acts
crackling into my veins
from face or body
or sound of creatures known before.
I roar and murmur
with their messages.

And similarly, now, out of me here, each
deed, word, thought
rockets its dots and dashes
into lives I encounter,
which later will snap
and flash on other globes in distant climes
more wisely, beautifully conceived for pure
communication.

The Whale

By that sea and that motion
past the traffic's last sob,
the gulls' slack elation
hung over brown ebb;

and there a whale's fortress
huge-flippered and sprung
from the anvils of duress
out of deep walls of song,

lay grisly-beaming
from eyes tall with death.
I saw Jesus slow-leaning
to the forehead's vast wreath,

and touching it silent
as though a saint's thought
moved calf-like and errant
in that kingdom of salt.

He smiled; that humped blackness
shone over our eyes;
the traffic's dull sickness
fell forward and lay

in the worms of the brine,
and the lighthouse of men
slid forward to die
in a blindness of stone.

The Line of the Sun

A black line along
the wall. The sun going.
I sought my mother's breathing.
She was gone.

I found my father
near. He watched with calm gaze.
"Light goes out in many ways,
anywhere,

any time," he said.
"But that is not the end
of the world." His words made sound
warm as blood,

of deep, simple tone.
"All right," I said. The room
rolled back. I blazed like a dark flame
gladdened by wind.

The Subliminal Jesus

I saw the Jesus stone
lathed at the hip of wood,
I felt the circular bone
revolve in the blood.

A thousand fiery stars
wheeled on the finger-tips,
and hunger masked with gore
sucked love-warm lips.

And there the water swung
from Jesus' neck
in rivers icy numb
as passion's shock;

I tried the turbulent bird,
the flying throat of sun,
that Jesus cried aloud
with gristle of pain.

And sweat like soil emerged
at my garden of pores,
and tall I grew and purged
by my green lives before;

and green and savage I teemed
with the eyes of animal dark
that nearer shuddered and flamed
with the unities death evoked,
the altar, the brotherly drum.

Devotional

If I lay
naked in snow
among women fully clothed,
would my loathsome guilt
be forgiven?

If I came there
blameless with striving
for a life redeemed,
would I find
the food of their cold
the last
true passion
of the enduring?

Oh, lovers in the grassy
winter white,
the blind drifts over the flesh
ready to be entered; I know the lean
cruel Master of that house,
the curse of endings
that I bless,
the messenger, the just
wonder of his rage
making my salvation from the blood and humus
of unreplying
thigh and hip and breast,

the icy mansion
where my black blight passes
and my life again is tall,
expelling the storms,
the welling words of nobler lust.

Sacrament

The frame of Jesus, spun of grass,
leaned up in wind, urged up in dust,
and broke across my portalled eyes
with the sure fist of rust.

Take hold, then, ore and weight of death,
crack forth earth's caravan of flame,
each insect-savior ticking my breath
into the praising name.

For what I speak is the vein's slash,
and what I keep blackens like roots.
Sun's tempest is my sharded flesh
from which I leap hot.

And gather, men, come closer to talk,
to cluster on my lips like lice;
each evil I savor for virtue's sake;
my brothers I utter best.

Dialogues with a Revolutionary Christ

"Are we to die?" I asked.

"Look at that coast," he answered. "You see
    the boulders moving,
yet no wind stirs: the boulders move in blood;
and over the surf that is the universe's love,
the birds, the birds men might have been are doing
the simple things men might have done."

"Like what?" I said.

"Pure yielding to the good. Pure giving.
Yes. You can see the wing-tips probing the air,
curved white most gentle, trusting, sure,
that learns direction by relaxed disdain of fear."

"Are we to die? And if so, when?"

"As men who suck the pus from festering machines,
who by those feral dead machines make profit's pus
on which they glut and which their blindness loves —
as these men eye the Orient whose storm
of fresher concept, mightier numbers, vaster power
towers over all time's dead ancestral forms,
crossing all man's ancient walls to scour
the sky with lightning of wild, fearless pride —
these Western pirate-scientists, exact
with brokers' 'progress,' security, and comfort's fact,
will fling the bomb of Holy Merchandise
to check the contemptible yellow maggot-race."

"And with the rest of us will die?"

"Precisely."

"What will death be like?"

> "Somewhat, I think, like gadgets wealth devised
> to dupe the lower-middle class into belief
> that they were potent, clever, rich, and somehow wise.
> Atomic pain will be a flash, a quick
> and superficial glitter the Power Elite
> will cry is photogenic, bargain-basement bright:
>
> " 'Only fifty million lost to win a world;
> Only time's end to murder atheism, do God's right!'
>
> Such death will be the slickness
> of automatic enamel mixing-bowls,
> the sterile glisten of costume jewelry."

"And will you take us, Christ — these retching souls
crammed to the gills with sewage of our age?"

> "Why not? I'm glad to clear the stage,
> to introduce a species worthier than man,
> truer to my law, to all I seek and am,
> like nature's creatures, innocent and clean,
> giving themselves to preserve and enjoy their own,
> blending in wisdom and purpose like wild geese across the sun,
> shifting yet cleaving, bound in a lucid
> intuitive flow and surge,
> a valorous, arrowy grace."

"And the earth, after cataclysm?"

"From the white abyss I shout.
From the cold caves of the umbilical land
I hammer the radiance to your hand;
I give you the power to pity and rout.

Again and again the earth yields;
it will break under atomic weight;
but primitive survivors will create,
the brotherly remnants will build."

"What can we do? Give us counsel, Christ."

"Take your weapons from the ancient wall,
the mercy that will hurl stone,
the terror shaped to the tough alone.
Stun society; make Goliath fall.

Destroy the scalpel of your mechanized time;
bury machines and drugs that taught fear;
in harmony's garden pick fierce flowers
to beautify the disciplined mind.

The trusting and plain can gather goods
for mutual love, defense, and ownership.
The praise of noble laws on your lips,
form structures of the clean and proud,

communities of interlacing blood
where power has ceased for nature's talk,
where Government is intuition's brawn,
labor is play, and all war dead."

part 3

The Flood

You have known, of course, that hill,
that rock from which the sun
is never seen as still,
but like a tormented one
moves through the writhing air
from dawn to evening star.

And on that peak a house,
and in that room a ceiling;
and there the water rose,
and hour by hour the failing
breath and heart felt water
push up the waist and shoulder

and press the head to ceiling
till only the mouth reached up
to suck that inch of whirling
air between darkness and hope.

Water ravaged the hill;
the sun was under water.
My weight was massive-cold;
it floated higher and tighter.
I heard the flood at the roof
and knew it was futile to strive.

In the attic, someone, however,
had left a radio running.
In announcing sports and weather,
cheerful, brisk, and sunny,

a vibrant voice made the wood
where my mouth touched, tremble. My blood

stirred. I held on longer,
much longer than I thought I could.
Finally, the water, far stronger
than I, closed the last
inch, but not before
I had heard the news, the best

values in suits, and the power
in the latest high-octane fuel.
Floating, submerged, I was told
of my superior lot.
I was thrilled to realize the hour,
my part in the mortal good,
the simple nature of thought,
the simple way to get
what I might need or want.

Martin Luther King

They say the whale
is failing, disappearing
from the seas, because of man's
ravaging, his insensate greed.

They say the eagle
bleeds his lofty final
life away because man loves
his guns' precision, sportsman's power.

They say that man
tracks down himself into
that doomed dark lair deep
beneath the rocks where in the past
he blasted out the fox and clubbed the frantic
rabbits to their death.

And yet, I saw
exalted glory, sable
as a whale, as fiercely strong,
that flung itself above the seas
of greed before it died, so nobly true
it hewed a deathless myth upon the sea and air.

I saw an eagle
rising steep and screaming,
as fearless as that past we thought
betrayed, as broad,
as godly high, serenely wise,
as our bright origins
long-dimming now.

I saw this vast, wing-beating bird
blot out the sun
with wonder man will not forget —
because it met the glare unthinkable,
the dazzle of sun itself with that straight stare
of rarest courage man is aware
he must achieve himself, or like the eagle
he will be
shot down.

Bag-Wall
(Christmas, 1965)

Dark, dark I said; let the bodies burn
atop a little wall, to light the pilots' way.
Thus are the hero fliers and their justice magnified,
their love explained;
and toys that downward float to lifted
                              infant skeleton hands
                              will dance
                              more clarified.

Bright, bright, the wall is flesh
                    and tall, and blood
                         crawls in the wrinkled skin
                              as in a lizard's wound;
the wall — a lumpy bag of leathered flesh,
in which the dying stir, and feebly thrust the shattered bone, the
     suffocating tongue upward
to closed
     openings.

And on this bag-wall burns
                    the further flesh
                         of elders — babies napalm-luminous —
cindery-sanctified by search-and-destroy,
the glow of pitying and Christian rain
                              sprayed scientific-flawlessly
to rot
the crops, spasm
     the cattle, decimate the trees.
                    All these, made tiny, jolly like a game,
shine in the holy warmth.

Tennis in the Forenoon

He has placed his cocktail glass
on a folded chair.
It is eleven o'clock.
No one knows how he found strength
to get up and be here.
But he likes to play
a little tight.

Stepping onto brick-dust court
watered, rolled, and chalked superbly right,
he claps brisk racket and elbow
in the way of ball
sent from a girl in shorts
whose legs and breasts
form hammock of familiar desire
spread like a tennis net.

Laughter accompanies her tanned bending,
her contrapuntals of angry grace and musical awe
probed and reverent as sun-adoring racial memory:
the wrist upon the top-spin turn, a hand
tilting a goblet to a temple sun;
the crouch for low volley: preparation of thigh
in phallic ritual.

Unable to attain her in any bed
too populated by those quicker,
he hopes in whirling forenoon, amid shots
skipping on powdered red
to navigate the white action
and rage of opened zipper.

After a sharp exchange,
protesting gasp, the glow of passing,
placing, making her over-reach,
he can walk to sideline,
lift glass, and through its liquid rearrange
the lines of conflict, obstacle, and sleek undressing.

And, having passed her the glass: "I'd like to teach
you how to whack
that backhand-overhead, one hand
behind your back!"

Her pretty screech!
And once again, the brick-dust, delicately damp
capturing sunlight whose love
sucks clean the failure of all flesh, bought face,
recurrent market-place.

The insolent ball, the court, the sheepgut combine
to sag him down at last,
to slow stroke, to caring less.
"Had enough? . . . You were sharp today! . . .
The good old sweat . . . That gin! . . .
No . . . leave it there:
the boy will take it back to the bar.
Now how about that swim?"

My Sister's Music

When the meadow below the wall has sunk to sleep,
the golden-rod died dusk-wise till another sun,
and hills warmer than a mother's arm
slipped outward to the ramparts of the moon;
when the tree beside the window says an old word
with shy nostalgia, murmurs, and grows still,
and late summer brushes close to people lonely and tired
with scent of melon, and apples fallen on grassy hill,

then, wandering alone in hallway, or on empty lawn,
wishing that birds of June might gild the dark
with their bright glory, finding the good friends gone
who raised with me the ladders to cloudy song —

then, all at once, slim as a current of air
that glides from damp grove into sweltering town,
the first notes of the piano lift and stir,
approach, over endless water where time drowns,
out of the lonely library where, yearning-alone,
my sister sits to search the trembling unknown.

And I am Arthur healed by a strange strength,
and I am Siegfried with his shield ablaze;
I am burdenless in invisible armor of coolness,
walking in dark with gnomes, no longer afraid,
striding from tunneled earth where roses burn,
to bathe my flesh in contentment for infinite days.

A Man I Hated

A man I hated
with a brave passion, stood
cowed, transfixed before me. Slowly,
with the motions of a poised and rational
man, I pulled him apart from the shoulders.
I tore him, raising him up.

Like a plucked, ripped
chicken, he lay in my hand.
Through the gap in his side
the bright beating of his heart was visible,
and all his organs flexed and hummed
and rubbed on one another with the usual
doings of life.

        And casually,
the man, though he lay in my palm,
went on talking,
talking with a friend
who bent forward, relaxed, to observe
the workings of the organs inside.

Amiable now, I gazed
through the open
door of the chicken carcass, studying
the details with the man's friend,
who leaned forward as I did, watching
the organs running.

The Gangster

The gangster, good-natured, kneeling
on clean grass,
was blasting at some object running along
the base of a wall.
He shot
flawlessly,
with amiable ease.
                        And I
was lying in the line of fire.

But what was travelling along
the wall? What life
was he firing at?

It was invisible.

And I lay nerveless,
observed by all my friends —
helpless, waiting for the bullets
to reach
the clean pouch
of my flesh
where the letters of all my loves
and hopes lay
waiting
to be written.

The Judge

The judge I cut with the razor of noon.
I drew the air of dead law from his brain.
Laying him cold on books and newsprint,
I bent a ray of truth into his blood.

Whenever the police sprang from blank walls,
I folded them stiff as sandpaper, and scrubbed
the judge's skin till a pink of health emerged.
I purged and scoured his waxen abdomen
to flatness. Then I heard the hornets of bells
spilling from the towers of civil authority.
These I placed on the judge's closed lids,
the thick, aching welt of his mouth,
to crowd the last sigh back with buzzing
of lovelessness, to sting the soul
to swollen-full with venom
of precedent, and evidence, and tract.

The facts, the busy correctness he'd spoken
floated and swarmed within his rancid bone,
bloated him to gelid, insensible shame.

The chamber of the law grew dark; I shouted
proud, different truths no one had heard before,
the clear announcement of my single, great decision.

A Place of Construction

Why, in that damp flatness, in that dirt I was there,
is a strange question; and of course, nobody cared;
and sensing that nobody cared, I was afraid.
I was completely alarmed at the circumstances and place.

I was alone, and it appeared to be a scooped-out depth
for a house foundation. But there was something close over my
     head
— boards or steel, — and around the edge of the flat square
a bulldozer kept scooping a trench deeper and deeper.

The place seemed familiar yet odd. I knew changes
were being made. I was at home with the old, but not the new
     ways.
I tried to explain this to a workman. I apologized. "Although,"
I said, "I am the one that's lost, I refuse to appeal to you."

He answered by coming in menacingly
at a front door still being built. "It seems to me,"
he declared, "that you should have been helped by the police,
and therefore, in the first place, should never have been lost."

And he came at me with a switch-knife, or it might have been
a broken bottle. I couldn't be sure; my brain
had snapped shut on the single thought that he was terribly angry;
and I cried out suddenly: "How impossible it is to explain!"

Television Nightfall

Last night by houses dying in rain,
past television sets aglow,
I walked toward sunset sky aflame
with a long scar through fleshy blue.

The road wound darkening toward a sea
of trees drowned in a clutch of hills.
In every house the watchers leaned
like mute insane whose lips are chilled;

in every house, in every room,
the stiffened, crouching listener.
Out through their walls their last thoughts flew
like shades of bleak and pitiful birds,

like skeletons of birds that rushed
from the skull's cold, from nesting numb;
past me they sped with sorrow's hiss,
beaks open, and their tongues were blood.

The Fence Adjoining Myself

One thing I ought to make clear:
That snow-piled fence is not out there,
with myself back here;
rather, it takes up *all* the space
between there, wherever that is, and my face,
and then proceeds into my skull and out behind.

Actually, it's a solid quantity
right through and past and on forever;
it is solid, and plane, and angle,
and plausible color;
yet that wood, that cold dazzle
must be not only far, but near,
and through all the intermediate stages as well.

Therefore, do not speak of that snow-heaped fence as apart,
or alien to touch and knowledge;
it's the bulge and valve of heart;
this brilliant winter day
is all things that move between —
meeting — ecstatic, identical, crushed through my skin.

My Friend, the Doctor

My naked foot was sheeted with blood,
a brilliant, glistening glaze.
But I felt nothing.
Nevertheless, anxious, I sent a little girl
for the doctor.

I saw him; he was a friend of mine.
He came leisurely down the long street,
with a coterie of companions. They were dressed up,
costly, and clean. They took their time.

I stood with numb and mutilated foot. Casually
he examined it. But he could not tell me what
had done it, or what to do. I suddenly realized
I had walked a long way. It was odd.
I had no sense of pain.

The clean, bright faces of all the doctor's friends
bent toward me like a circle of flowers.
Powerless, I stood with the foot half lifted
and stiffening in its glaze of blood.
And the lovely-apparelled, well-to-do people watched.

Driving to Class

I drove to work on a vacuum cleaner.
The speed was unsatisfactory; but I gripped
the slick, black, long wired post at an exact
angle, well away from me, like the prop
of a harp, and with the efficiency of an executive,
pressed the switch for speed.

The trees moved by slowly. I had
a class to teach at 8 P.M. I became
impatient.

      Then,
as I entered a paved road
broad and new and ready for a speed
of at least fifteen miles per hour, I came to sawhorses
across an intersection. A cop, hand raised,
gazed at me stonily.

                "Repair work. You can't
pass here."

        Panicked, I turned
the whirring vacuum cleaner, gripped
the switch for top speed,
leaned forward atavistically.

                  But abruptly, horribly,
I stalled! Now — I'd never
get there by eight.
But wait! Rolling

down a slope, I threw in the clutch, drew
the shifting-lever into second, then
let the clutch out suddenly.

                       The motor caught.
My heart sprang free and valorous again. I fled
at a fresh, astonishing speed up a hill
bristling with traffic — weaving in and out,
flouting all rules, doing at least twenty-five.

I'd arrive now, on time; I knew it.
I was sure — absolutely — with a certainty
verging on insolence.

My Father's Head

My father's head was off,
but he was living normally.
And then, as I watched,
his head became that of a horse.
And, most peculiar, he was praying;
his hands were uplifted.

Why did he act that way?
Didn't he realize that the gifted,
quiet, religious kinds of people
had to retain their identity? —
and that a horse, after all, wasn't able
to clasp his hands together; in fact,
it was really questionable
whether a horse would even have hands.

Pittsburgh Worker

In the slashed harmony, the orchestra blaze
of light from open blast-furnace door,
amoeba-workman clings, naked and unicellular,
most beautifully pitted against the molten rage
of earth and air
and blind death everywhere.

His harmony, his melted eye and wrought bone
catch every shock for me, temper my need.
Alone, he builds cathedral tone
out of cauldron's white anger;
the steel of his flesh will raise,
will arch my praise
in objects giving ease
for gentleness and wonder.

Steel-worker, I saw you hurled, held,
flesh-human blossom against the storm
of heat;
thrust there, primitive-joyed, in spell
of sacrificial music-beat,
the sacred sweat that I may be more calm,
more safe and strictly neat
in chair, or bed, or speeding chasmed street.

The singed sheaf of your skin, the crisp
strength-beauty sliced from core
I grow in gardens of my leisured wish,
refinement's fragrant flower.

Conversation with a Friend

My friend, the talks I have with you
are that bright orchard snarl of limbs
I stole through as a thieving boy
for the crab-apple's crimply taste,
knob-pithy pinkness yielding strict
and bitter beauty of stolen feast.

Thus from the harsh and canny yield
of your life's webbing stamped by sun
I filch those stingy mercies full
which grant a quick and acid power
the juices of my heart can turn
through all the branches of my year.

Relaxed, conversing, we make our air
an orchard texture of woven word,
the august from sullen, wit from dour,
gladness from both. Yet all the while
I sense a watcher, that boyhood curse,
the neighbor-owner; and this one smiles

as lemon-taut, as pronged with stare
as she in window, frail and fierce,
who watched, fingering the glass with mild
and childish hands. And this is decay —
mortality, who owns and peers.

Modern Theatre, Uninhibited

The theatre has become,
      has suddenly become a place
           of faces unbecoming and defiled
                by smiles
of quaint urbanity which seem
          to squeeze
a toothpaste of unbreathing death,
          of breathless choking out of the tube
               of blue-lipped
               salesmanship.
In this new theatre of America's fine
          unbridled sexually happy
             drama,
I can taste the palatable and white,
          the soft, bright
               lightness, foaminess of paste
               that must,
oh must be cleansing something out,
          be routing forth the scraps
               of those unhappy
               animals of past
               old-fashioned
loves and values who died
          inside my mouth in bites
             of life
             assigned to dark decay
between my teeth or in the gray moist rubber-gloves
               of my loveless entrails,
               failing
deeper as they're squeezed to sordiness of human waste.

And so this paste
of happy, tawdry, sexy theatre must be
                        flushing out something sick
                                and bitter, something
                                unessential
or indecent.
            I squeeze the tube and brush and spit into the bowl
                                and whirl
the foamy white away.

            So gaily is my every failing rinsed and cleansed,
                            and breath
made sexually fair, And yet I cannot find
                        just why I need this brushing,
                            just what
those failings were, what is being sluiced away that could
                            be food
or recently-living matter. All I taste is the sweet
                                unbreathing prophylactic
                                valueless
substance priced beyond reason.
                All I'm feeling is the foam
which makes me retch
        with emptiness.

The First Gallop

Taken onto a horse,
forced forward into the trail,
I bent my head,
I said what children should.

But the branches beat
raw sweetness into my brain,
a rain of green whisked
the blissful foam of thrush-song

over my breast.
And I gladly went down;
I strung the bones
of the animal to mine,

and blithely felt the hooves
love me to thunder,
to wonder and savage grief
of the adult.

I sank along the floor
of roaring fear, the pace,
the savor of wisdom
wrung in sweat,

till jolt of stopping
by rocks as huge as towers
flowered me into words,
the thirsty-lost, the dimpled
in wisdom for all time,

like chiming thrush,
like rush of beast's volition.

My lungs flailed outward
with sound too big for lips:
"I did it! I did it!" —

accents too huge for me
or any age. I struck
his neck with fists, leaped
to the fierce, black rock
to shock my feet and sinew,

to beat me out of timeless,
back to the child I'd been.

The Sound

In whatever room
I stood, strangely expectant,
I heard a sudden
rushing crash of sound, some accident
fast and final. Had some object
been dropped?
           I knew
I would die
in the fire. There was no way
to see, to get out, for darkness
stark and consuming enfolded the soft
clotted pectin
of my flesh
like a wet mouth pressing a grape.
In the flames about to break forth I would waver
and fail like a breathing
seed.

The Old Maid Walks
by the Graveyard

The graves she peopled with life.
She had none of her own.
Each grave she shaped into love —
a warm chamber of stone,
where the embrace she never had won
would be sun-flesh and brawn.

Each day from her silent house
she set forth with her dog
toward hilltop of sycamore voice
and sumac flag,
or the locust's icy praise
of the seablown fog.

Only the dog heard her speak,
light words — hiding prayer;
he too went earth-down deep
on a lonely stair,
and peopled the rooms beneath
with desirous fur —
the wild play lost to him here.

Sad mortal and animal thought
communion-blended, devout.

In the train
    the lane between
        people reading was as broad
as a hot desert separating two dying, thirsty towns.
                  And down
into importunate ads and magazine sex
          that breathlessly tall forests had died to disseminate
on pages glossy as the brow of death — down into this
the eyes corkscrewed hard. Baldness and plump hand
                   swam there in dusty
suffocating light. Till, shouting pleasure,
          the Master broke
the window glass, fed them
the fury of song, sudden nature's power,
             roaring wood and river unfurling
from where air poured.

        The train spun,
flung them, singing and drinking freshness, into
              the city's tunnel
where the walls
      awed to radiance
drew back.

      I brought the train to a stop, and with the Master's aid,
led the apotheosized and stunned
into a Grand Central Station as broad and flowering as the
            meadows of Yellowstone.

acknowledgments

American Dialog: PITTSBURGH WORKER; THE FLOOD. *American Weave:* TELEVISION NIGHTFALL; TO AN ANCIENT LADY I LOVED. *Chicago Tribune:* FROM THE FIELDS BELOW; KINGBIRDS TOPPLE BACKWARD. *Coastlines:* THE FIRST GALLOP. *Colorado Quarterly:* YOUNG MARRIAGE AND THE SKI-RUN. *Dimension:* THE EXAMINATION. *Freelance:* THE MEAT. *The Humanist:* THE LINE OF THE SUN. *The Literary Review:* A CHRONICLE OF PRAYER. *Lynx:* THE SOUND. *Minority of One:* MODERN THEATRE; COMMUTER TRAIN. *New Mexico Quarterly:* MY FATHER'S DEATH. *New Poetry Pamphlets:* THE FLOOD; THE LAMB; THE GANGSTER. *The New Republic:* THE JUDGE. *New York Herald-Tribune:* THE FENCE ADJOINING MYSELF; FRAIL IS THAT ROAD; YOUR PROFILE IN THIS DESPERATE HOUR; THE WHALE. *New York Times:* CONVERSATION WITH A FRIEND. *Northeast:* SACRAMENT. *Prairie Schooner:* A MAN I HATED; THE CATERPILLAR. *Renaissance:* OCTOBER'S END; A ROMAN IN THE OAK. *The Smith:* BAG-WALL; DEVOTIONAL; THE FERNS BENEATH. *The Southwest Review:* TENNIS IN THE FORENOON; SUMMER DECISION; THE NATURAL MAN AND THE INSTRUMENT PANEL; THE LARK AND THE ASTER. *The Sparrow:* THE MORTAL TRAVELLER. *Trace:* MY FATHER'S HEAD. *Voices:* MESSIAH; MY SISTER'S MUSIC. *Whetstone:* DRIVING TO CLASS; WHAT KEEPS THE LOVERS IN THE TREES BELOW; THE SUBLIMINAL JESUS.